RACHE'

# Perfect Peace

### planting my eyes on Jesus

## BIBLE READING PLAN
## & JOURNAL

PERFECT PEACE
Bible Reading Plan and Journal
PUBLISHED BY RACHEL WOJO
Copyright © 2017 by Rachel Wojnarowski

Visit **www.rachelwojo.com/shop**

Requests for information should be addressed to rachel@rachelwojo.com

Trade Paperback ISBN  (Rachel Wojo LLC)
ISBN-ISBN-13: 978-0692849224
ISBN-10: 069284922X

Cover design by Rachel Wojnarowski

Photo credit: Bigstock.com

Library of Congress Cataloging-in-Publication Data

Printed in the United States of America
2017—First Edition--1001

# Table of Contents

# Table of Contents

# A Personal Note from Rachel

Dear Friend,

Thank you for joining in to enjoy a restorative journey for perfect peace. My goal through Bible reading is to draw closer to Jesus, and I want that for you too!

Through reading daily Bible passages, praying, and listening to God, we're going to nurture and grow our relationship with him. This Bible reading plan and journal is specifically focused on true peace that only comes from Jesus.

In an ever-striving world, the eyes of our hearts can easily lose focus. When we center on Jesus, his peace envelops our souls and radiates from our spirits.

I'm craving the kind of tranquility that extends beyond human comprehension. You too? This Bible reading plan will remind us that when we plant our eyes on Jesus, we discover perfect peace.

I.can't.wait!

Rachel

## Planting My Eyes On Jesus

Welcome to the Perfect Peace Journal. I'm so excited to begin this journey with you! For the next thirty-one days, we are going to dig into God's word and grow closer to Him. Together we'll make the choice to fix our eyes on Jesus by reading his word and applying it in our daily lives.

> The best gifts are typically wrapped inside of hearts rather than paper....Peace? Ah, peace is such a gift.
> --*One More Step*

Are you ready to unwrap the gift of peace as we walk this path of Scripture together? You can share what you are learning on social media by using the hashtags #perfectpeacejournal and #biblereadingplan or you can just keep it between you and God.

# 4 Simple Steps to Growing in Faith

## Step 1:

Pray: Spend some time with God in prayer. Prayer is simply having a conversation with him.

## Step 2:

Read the Bible passage for the day one time slowly, soaking in each phrase. Read again if time allows.

## Step 3:

Answer the daily question.

## Step 4:

Complete the journaling section.

Psalm 29:1-11

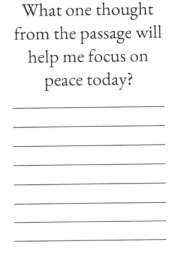

# Blessing

Peace is a blessing
from the Lord.

What one thought
from the passage will
help me focus on
peace today?

_____
_____
_____
_____
_____
_____
_____
_____

## Peaceful Reflections

Describe a time when you experienced God's peace in your
life or observed it in someone else's life.

_____
_____
_____
_____
_____
_____
_____
_____
_____
_____
_____
_____
_____

# Justified

I have peace with
God because of
Jesus.

When I'm feeling
overwhelmed, what
fact about Jesus
would deliver peace?

_____
_____
_____
_____
_____
_____
_____
_____

## Peaceful Reflections

Describe a peaceful place you've visited or imagined and
reflect on the feelings you experienced there. Thank Jesus
that his peace can be experienced right where you are!

_____
_____
_____
_____
_____
_____
_____
_____
_____
_____
_____
_____
_____

Psalm 37:10-19

# Meekness

Pride is the very
thing that often
prevents peace.

Where have I
searched for peace in
place of Jesus?

_____
_____
_____
_____
_____
_____
_____
_____

## Peaceful Reflections

Can you recall a time when your choices did not promote
peace? Tell God about it and ask for forgiveness.

_____
_____
_____
_____
_____
_____
_____
_____
_____
_____
_____
_____

Peace
in my heart
is not
*dependent*
on others'
actions;
peace is
*dependent*
on my heart's
content.

Proverbs 16:1-7

# Crave

Where have I
searched for peace in
place of Jesus?

The best way to
carry peace in our
hearts is to stay
close with the
Peacemaker.

_____
_____
_____
_____
_____
_____
_____
_____

## Day 4

## Peaceful Reflections

Can you recall a time when your choices did not promote
peace? Tell God about it and ask for forgiveness.

_____
_____
_____
_____
_____
_____
_____
_____
_____
_____
_____

Psalm 4:1-8

# Listen

In the quiet, I can rest in peace and hear God speak to my heart.

When I'm feeling overwhelmed, what fact about Jesus would deliver peace?

_____

_____

_____

_____

_____

_____

_____

_____

## Peaceful Reflections

Describe a time when you experienced God's peace in your life or observed it in someone else's life.

_____

_____

_____

_____

_____

_____

_____

_____

_____

_____

_____

_____

_____

Job 5:17-27

# Ponder

Reflecting on God's peace in the past reassures peace in the future.

What one thought from the passage will help me focus on peace today?

_____

_____

_____

_____

_____

_____

_____

_____

_____

## Peaceful Reflections

Describe a peaceful place you've visited or imagined and reflect on the feelings you experienced there. Thank Jesus that his peace can be experienced right where you are!

_____

_____

_____

_____

_____

_____

_____

_____

_____

_____

_____

Psalm 120:1-7

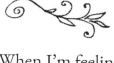

# Journey

God answers my
prayers requesting
peace.

When I'm feeling
overwhelmed, what
fact about Jesus
would deliver peace?

_____

_____

_____

_____

_____

_____

_____

## Peaceful Reflections

Describe a time when you experienced God's peace in your
life or observed it in someone else's life.

_____

_____

_____

_____

_____

_____

_____

_____

_____

_____

_____

_____

# Assured

When things
seem out of
control, God is
always in control.
-One More Step

When I'm feeling
overwhelmed, what
fact about Jesus
would deliver peace?

_____
_____
_____
_____
_____
_____
_____

## Peaceful Reflections

Describe a peaceful place you've visited or imagined and
reflect on the feelings you experienced there. Thank Jesus
that his peace can be experienced right where you are!

_____
_____
_____
_____
_____
_____
_____
_____
_____
_____
_____
_____

Psalm 85:1-13

## Hear

Our Father voices
peace
incomprehensible.

Where have I
searched for peace in
place of Jesus?

_____
_____
_____
_____
_____
_____
_____
_____
_____
_____

## Peaceful Reflections

Can you recall a time when your choices did not promote
peace? Tell God about it and ask for forgiveness.

_____
_____
_____
_____
_____
_____
_____
_____
_____
_____
_____
_____
_____
_____

Loving God & Others
+
Being Faithful
+
Doing Right
=
**Peace**

# Proverbs 3:13-22

## Establish

Wisdom walks
in peace.

When I'm feeling
overwhelmed, what
fact about Jesus
would deliver peace?

_____
_____
_____
_____
_____
_____
_____

## Peaceful Reflections

Describe a time when you experienced God's peace in your
life or observed it in someone else's life.

_____
_____
_____
_____
_____
_____
_____
_____
_____
_____
_____
_____

Isaiah 9:1-7

# Celebrate

The Prince of
Peace longs to
reign in our
hearts in every
season of life.

What one thought
from the passage will
help me focus on
peace today?

_____
_____
_____
_____
_____
_____
_____
_____
_____

## Peaceful Reflections

Describe a peaceful place you've visited or imagined and
reflect on the feelings you experienced there. Thank Jesus
that his peace can be experienced right where you are!

_____
_____
_____
_____
_____
_____
_____
_____
_____
_____
_____
_____
_____

John 14:23-31

Jesus gives peace
the world cannot
offer.

When I'm feeling
overwhelmed, what
fact about Jesus
would deliver peace?

_____
_____
_____
_____
_____
_____
_____
_____
_____

## Peaceful Reflections

Describe a time when you experienced God's peace in your
life or observed it in someone else's life.

_____
_____
_____
_____
_____
_____
_____
_____
_____
_____
_____
_____

# Focus

Jesus keeps me in
perfect peace
when I trust in
His word.

Where have I
searched for peace in
place of Jesus?

_____
_____
_____
_____
_____
_____
_____
_____

## Peaceful Reflections

Describe a peaceful place you've visited or imagined and
reflect on the feelings you experienced there. Thank Jesus
that his peace can be experienced right where you are!

_____
_____
_____
_____
_____
_____
_____
_____
_____
_____
_____

When I
remain
focused
on God,
He keeps
my heart
at peace.

Proverbs 12:15-23

## Intentional

Being a peace-planner will bring joy to my heart.

What one thought from the passage will help me focus on peace today?

_____
_____
_____
_____
_____
_____
_____
_____
_____

## Peaceful Reflections

Describe a time when you experienced God's peace in your life or observed it in someone else's life.

_____
_____
_____
_____
_____
_____
_____
_____
_____
_____
_____
_____
_____
_____

2 Thess. 1:1-12

# Grace

Giving grace is
often the
beginning of
peacemaking.

What one thought
from the passage will
help me focus on
peace today?

_____
_____
_____
_____
_____
_____
_____
_____
_____

## Peaceful Reflections

Can you recall a time when your choices did not promote
peace? Tell God about it and ask for forgiveness.

_____
_____
_____
_____
_____
_____
_____
_____
_____
_____
_____
_____
_____
_____

Psalm 39:1-13

I must search for peace in the person of Christ rather than places of my choosing.

Where have I searched for peace in place of Jesus?

_____
_____
_____
_____
_____
_____
_____
_____

## Peaceful Reflections

Describe a peaceful place you've visited or imagined and reflect on the feelings you experienced there. Thank Jesus that his peace can be experienced right where you are!

_____
_____
_____
_____
_____
_____
_____
_____
_____
_____
_____
_____
_____
_____

Jesus
is
my
hope
and
peace.

# Accountability

Maintaining a position of peacekeeping isn't always an easy task.

What one thought from the passage will help me focus on peace today?

_____

_____

_____

_____

_____

_____

_____

_____

## Peaceful Reflections

Can you recall a time when your choices did not promote peace? Tell God about it and ask for forgiveness.

_____

_____

_____

_____

_____

_____

_____

_____

_____

_____

_____

_____

# Pursue

I must choose to
focus on building
up even when I
feel like tearing
down.

What one thought
from the passage will
help me focus on
peace today?

_____
_____
_____
_____
_____
_____
_____
_____

## Peaceful Reflections

Describe a time when you experienced God's peace in your
life or observed it in someone else's life.

_____
_____
_____
_____
_____
_____
_____
_____
_____
_____
_____
_____

# Petition

Peace is a result of prayer.

What one thought from the passage will help me focus on peace today?

_____
_____
_____
_____
_____
_____
_____
_____
_____

## Peaceful Reflections

Describe a peaceful place you've visited or imagined and reflect on the feelings you experienced there. Thank Jesus that his peace can be experienced right where you are!

_____
_____
_____
_____
_____
_____
_____
_____
_____
_____
_____
_____
_____
_____

Isaiah 54:1-10

# Compassion

The Lord will not remove His covenant of peace from me.

When I'm feeling overwhelmed, what fact about Jesus would deliver peace?

_____
_____
_____
_____
_____
_____
_____
_____

## Peaceful Reflections

Describe a peaceful place you've visited or imagined and reflect on the feelings you experienced there. Thank Jesus that his peace can be experienced right where you are!

_____
_____
_____
_____
_____
_____
_____
_____
_____
_____
_____
_____

Romans 15:1-13

# Filled

Trusting God
promotes peace.

What one thought
from the passage will
help me focus on
peace today?

_____
_____
_____
_____
_____
_____
_____
_____
_____

## Peaceful Reflections

Describe a time when you experienced God's peace in your
life or observed it in someone else's life.

_____
_____
_____
_____
_____
_____
_____
_____
_____
_____
_____
_____
_____

## Peace Promoting Plan

Build up my neighbor.

Hope in God's Word.

Live in harmony with others.

Philippians 4:1-7

## Follow

His truth
preserves our
peace.

Where have I
searched for peace in
place of Jesus?

_____
_____
_____
_____
_____
_____
_____
_____

## Peaceful Reflections

Describe a peaceful place you've visited or imagined and
reflect on the feelings you experienced there. Thank Jesus
that his peace can be experienced right where you are!

_____
_____
_____
_____
_____
_____
_____
_____
_____
_____
_____
_____

I cannot
fathom
God's ways
in totality.
His peace
exceeds
all
understanding.

Isaiah 55:1-13

# Relationship

Peace results when the Prince of Peace reigns in my heart.

When I'm feeling overwhelmed, what fact about Jesus will deliver peace?

_____
_____
_____
_____
_____
_____
_____
_____

## Peaceful Reflections

Describe a time when you experienced God's peace in your life or observed it in someone else's life.

_____
_____
_____
_____
_____
_____
_____
_____
_____
_____
_____
_____

If I believe that peace will be
achieved
when I understand
everything God is doing
or how He is working,
then peace will only be waiting for
me in heaven.
Jesus, please hold my heart
according to your promises.

Matt. 5:1-12

# Obedience

Living by God's
word brings peace
and happiness to
my heart.

Where have I
searched for peace in
place of Jesus?

_____
_____
_____
_____
_____
_____
_____
_____
_____

## Peaceful Reflections

Can you recall a time when your behavior did not promote
peace? Tell God about it and ask for forgiveness.

_____
_____
_____
_____
_____
_____
_____
_____
_____
_____
_____
_____
_____
_____

2 Cor. 13:7-14

# Strive

Living in peace
requires effort.

What one thought
from the passage will
help me focus on
peace today?

_____
_____
_____
_____
_____
_____
_____
_____

## Peaceful Reflections

Can you recall a time when your behavior did not promote
peace? Tell God about it and ask for forgiveness.

Aim for restoration.

*Comfort one another.*

Agree with one another.

*Live in peace.*

Psalm 119:161-168

# Day 26

## Promise

When I take God at His word, I can have great peace.

When I'm feeling overwhelmed, what fact about Jesus would deliver peace?

_____
_____
_____
_____
_____
_____
_____
_____
_____

## Peaceful Reflections

Describe a time when you experienced God's peace in your life or observed it in someone else's life.

_____
_____
_____
_____
_____
_____
_____
_____
_____
_____
_____
_____

James 3:10-18

# Pure

Wisdom produces
peace.

What one thought
from the passage will
help me focus on
peace today?

_____
_____
_____
_____
_____
_____
_____
_____
_____

## Peaceful Reflections

Describe a peaceful place you've visited or imagined and
reflect on the feelings you experienced there. Thank Jesus
that his peace can be experienced right where you are!

_____
_____
_____
_____
_____
_____
_____
_____
_____
_____
_____
_____
_____

# Purpose

Life and peace is
obtained by
setting my mind
on the spirit.

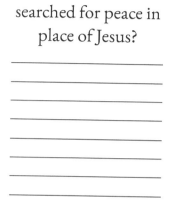

Where have I
searched for peace in
place of Jesus?

_____

_____

_____

_____

_____

_____

_____

_____

_____

## Peaceful Reflections

Describe a time when you experienced God's peace in your
life or observed it in someone else's life.

_____

_____

_____

_____

_____

_____

_____

_____

_____

_____

_____

_____

Proverbs 16:17

# Simple

Obedience to
God brings peace.

What one thought
from the passage will
help me focus on
peace today?

_____

_____

_____

_____

_____

_____

_____

_____

_____

## Peaceful Reflections

Can you recall a time when your choices did not promote
peace? Tell God about it and ask for forgiveness.

_____

_____

_____

_____

_____

_____

_____

_____

_____

_____

_____

_____

_____

In the search for peace,
I must first yield myself to the
Author of Peace.

John 16:21-33

# Overcomer

Jesus grounds my
frantic heart like
no one or nothing
else can.

When I'm feeling
overwhelmed, what
fact about Jesus
would deliver peace?

_____
_____
_____
_____
_____
_____
_____
_____

## Peaceful Reflections

Describe a time when you experienced God's peace in your
life or observed it in someone else's life.

_____
_____
_____
_____
_____
_____
_____
_____
_____
_____
_____
_____
_____
_____

Colossians 3:12-17

# Day 31

## Thanksgiving

A thankful heart
reaps peace.

What one thought
from the passage will
help me focus on
peace today?

_____
_____
_____
_____
_____
_____
_____
_____
_____

## Peaceful Reflections

Describe a peaceful place you've visited or imagined and
reflect on the feelings you experienced there. Thank Jesus
that his peace can be experienced right where you are!

_____
_____
_____
_____
_____
_____
_____
_____
_____
_____
_____

# Put a Bow on It!

You did it! You read your Bible for 31 days in a row!

Experience the peace of God through Jesus Christ is a blessing and a privilege. I pray that as you've walked this 31-day path, you've encountered a peace beyond human understanding.

*Peace! peace! wonderful peace,*
*Coming down from the Father above;*
*Sweep over my spirit forever, I pray,*
*In fathomless billows of love.*
*Wonderful Peace hymn*
*WD Cornell*

My prayer is that this Bible reading plan and journaling experience has enabled your mind and soul to embrace the peace only Christ offers.

Thanks for joining me on this journey through the Bible. Discover more Bible reading plans & journals at rachelwojo.com/shop.

# About the Author

Rachel "Wojo" Wojnarowski is wife to Matt and mom to seven wonderful kids. Her greatest passion is inspiring others to welcome Jesus into their lives and enjoy the abundant life he offers.

As a sought-after blogger and writer, she sees thousands of readers visit her blog daily. Rachel leads community ladies' Bible studies in central Ohio and serves as an event planner and speaker. In her "free time" she crochets, knits, and sews handmade clothing. Okay, not really. She enjoys running and she's a tech geek at heart.

Reader, writer, speaker, and dreamer, Rachel can be found on her website at **www.RachelWojo.com**.

## Free Bible Study Video Series

If you enjoyed this Bible reading plan & journal, then you'll love Rachel's free video Bible study to help you find strength for difficult seasons of life! **http://rachelwojo.com/free-bible-study-video-series-for-one-more-step/**

# Feel like giving up?

Are you ready to quit? Give up? But deep down, you want to figure out how to keep on keeping on?

Like you, Rachel has faced experiences that crushed her dreams of the perfect life: a failed marriage, a daughter's heartbreaking diagnosis, and more. In this book, she transparently shares her pain and empathizes with yours, then points you to the path of God's Word, where you'll find hope to carry you forward. One More Step gives you permission to ache freely—and helps you believe that life won't always be this hard. No matter the circumstances you face, through these pages you'll learn to...

- persevere through out-of-control circumstances and gain a more intimate relationship with Jesus
- run to God's Word when discouragement strikes
- replace feelings of despair with truths of Scripture

BUY NOW
www.rachelwojo.com/onemorestep

If you enjoyed this Bible reading plan and journal, then you'll love:

45995503R00032

Made in the USA
San Bernardino, CA
23 February 2017